RESCUE!

RESCUE!

TRUE STORIES OF HEROISM

by L. B. Taylor, Jr.

ILLUSTRATED BY
MICHAEL DEAS

FRANKLIN WATTS
NEW YORK ☐ LONDON ☐ 1978

Library of Congress Cataloging in Publication Data

Taylor, L   B
    Rescue!

    SUMMARY: Relates the exploits of teenagers
who were awarded the Carnegie Hero Fund Commission's medal of honor for their heroic efforts at
saving lives.
    1.   United   States—Biography—Juvenile litera-
ture.   2.   Heroes—United States—Biography—Juvenile literature.   3.   Youth—United States—Biography—Juvenile literature.   [1.   Heroes.   2.
United States—Biography]
I. Deas, Michael.   II.   Title.
CT217.T37   920′.073   78–3665
ISBN 0–531–02223–4

☐ This book is for my son, Tony

Contents

RESCUE!

1.

Rescue!

☐ It was a typical spring afternoon on April 29, 1974, in Durham, North Carolina. It was pleasantly warm, not muggy as it gets later, in the summer. Soft clouds scudded across the sky and a slight breeze was blowing as kids leisurely made their way home from school.

There was no hint of impending tragedy.

To Phil Williamson, sixty years old, it was just another workday. But he liked his job. Williamson drove an ice cream truck, and most of the kids smiled and waved at him as he passed them. But as he approached a railroad crossing, he was distracted for some reason and didn't see the long freight train coming down the tracks. Suddenly, he turned and froze in horror as the speeding engine bore down on him. But it was too late. His truck was already astride the tracks.

There was a terrible crash of grinding metal and glass as the train smashed into his truck, twisting its frame and knocking it down the tracks. The train's emergency brakes squealed loudly. The great crescendo of sound caused by the crash and the abrupt halting of the train died out as quickly as it had begun, and for a second or two there was an eerie silence.

Williamson was stunned and badly shaken by the

awful blow. He was alive, but blood was oozing down from his forehead, and his body felt as if some giant sledge-hammer had just banged him all over. He ached from head to foot. But his pain suddenly gave way to stark fear. Flames leaped up out of the front end of the truck and were fanning toward the cab. Williamson was afraid the flames would envelop him, or possibly spread to the truck's gas tank, triggering an explosion.

Frantically he tugged at the door handle, trying to get out, but it was badly bent and wouldn't open. He couldn't move. He was pinned in, trapped. The flames were getting nearer.

"Help!" he screamed. "Somebody help me." He didn't want to die in a blazing inferno.

Across the tracks, several people stood mute, almost in shock. They had heard the dreadful crash and had turned in time to see Williamson's truck being demolished. Then they saw the flames shoot up from the truck and heard his cries for help. Yet they still stood there, without moving, as if hypnotized.

One did not, though. Sixteen-year-old high school student William E. (Bill) Welch, Jr., instinctively bolted from the gathering crowd and ran toward the truck. Some of the kids shouted to him not to go, that the truck might explode, but he either didn't hear them or didn't pay attention.

As he reached the truck, the flames from the front end flared up, and more fire broke out from beneath the vehicle. The heat was intense, but Bill Welch didn't flinch. He yanked hard at the door, but it wouldn't budge. Then he reached inside the open window on the driver's side, threw his arms around Williamson, and began to pull. At first he couldn't move the heavier driver, but as the flames drew ever closer, Bill somehow found the strength to free

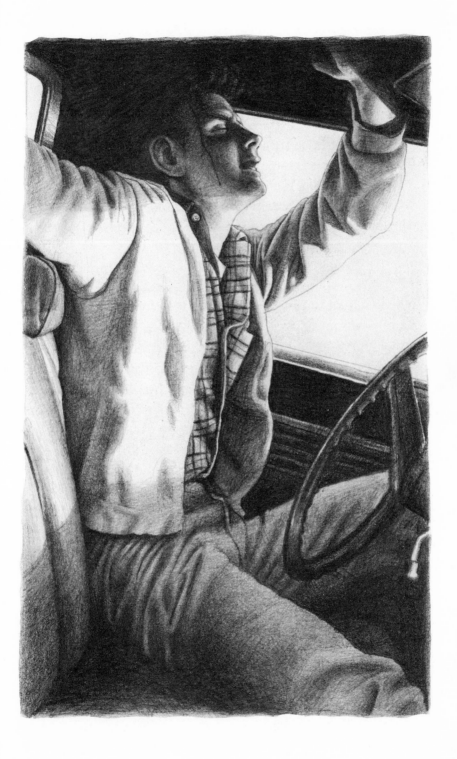

Williamson. Then, as sweat rolled down his face and the heat began to blister his skin, he pulled Williamson through the open window and dragged him away from the burning truck.

Stopping to rest a few yards away, Bill turned back and saw that the entire cab was now engulfed in the blaze, and a few seconds later the whole truck went up in flames.

Had not Bill Welch pulled him free, Phil Williamson would have met a horrible death trapped in his fiery truck cab. As it was, he soon recovered from his injuries.

☐ It was one of the first warm days of summer, June 17, 1972, in Duncansville, Pennsylvania, and for the kids, out of school only a few days, it was a great day for the motel swimming pool. There was splashing and laughing and running and diving and games of pool tag.

Thirteen-year-old Karen Edwards was enjoying herself. A good swimmer, she practiced her freestyle stroke for a while, and then got out of the pool to dry off and rest.

Eugene Taylor, a thirty-seven-year-old truck driver, was relaxing at poolside when he noticed his ten-year-old son had somehow gotten into the deep end of the pool and was struggling to stay above water. He couldn't swim. Taylor couldn't swim either, but he immediately jumped into the pool, trying to reach his son. Instead, however, he went under and did not surface.

Karen saw what was happening, and while others stood by, she ran to the deep end and dived in. She reached the boy quickly and towed him to the side of the pool, where others lifted him out. Then she swam back to where Taylor had gone under and was floating, face down, below the surface about thirteen feet from the side of the pool.

Taylor outweighed her by nearly one hundred

pounds, but Karen, summoning strength she didn't know she had, somehow managed to bring him to the surface, where both of them gasped for air. Treading water as she caught her breath, Karen started toward the edge of the pool, but Taylor, regaining consciousness, began flailing his arms in the water, sending up a shower of spray that momentarily blinded Karen, and she lost her hold on him.

Her chest heaving, Karen was nearly exhausted, but once again she reached for Taylor, grabbed him under his arms, and started for safety. Slowly, painfully, she worked toward the side, and finally, when she was close enough, someone held out a pool chair and she held on to it and was pulled to the side along with Taylor. Once out of the water, he quickly revived.

Had it not been for Karen's quick action, both Eugene Taylor and his son probably would have drowned.

2.

The Search for Heroes and Heroines

☐ Because they courageously risked their lives to save others, Bill Welch and Karen Edwards were awarded bronze medals by an organization in Pittsburgh called the Carnegie Hero Fund Commission.

Such medals, sometimes called the "Civilian Medal of Honor," are awarded annually by the commission to heroes and heroines all over the United States and Canada. The number of such awards may range anywhere from 50 to 150 or more per year, and many of them are presented to young people.

In fact, since the commission was founded in 1904, more than 6,000 individual awards for acts of heroism have been made, and more than $12 million has been distributed to the heroes and heroines and to the families of those who lost their lives in attempts to save others.

The cash awards are presented to medal winners who are not well off financially. Many such awards to boys and girls are used to help pay for their college educations.

The famous industrialist Andrew Carnegie, who helped develop some of the nation's earliest steel mills in the Pittsburgh area, founded the commission in 1904. Actually, Carnegie had been considering such an idea for a number of years. In one of his biographies it is written that he got his first inspiration for such a fund in 1886, when a young boy named William Hunter lost his life while trying to save two other boys from drowning in a lake in Carnegie's native Scotland.

Carnegie contributed money for a monument to Hunter bearing the following epitaph: "The false heroes of barbarous man are those who can only boast of the destruction of their fellows. The true heroes of civilization are those alone who save or greatly serve them. Young Hunter was one of those and deserves an enduring monument."

Eighteen years later, following the heroic deaths of two rescuers in a coal mine tragedy in Pennsylvania, Carnegie officially set up the commission with a $5 million endowment. He had long felt that while soldiers had always been decorated, honored, feted, and pensioned for killing other soldiers, there was no proper recognition for those whom he called the "heroes of peace."

Between 1908 and 1911 Carnegie established similar funds in Belgium, Denmark, France, Germany, Great Britain, Italy, the Netherlands, Norway, Sweden, and Switzerland. All but the German one are still in existence.

The medal, a little larger than a silver dollar, bears the likeness of Carnegie on the front. On the reverse is an inscribed quote from the New Testament, John 15:13, which reads: "Greater love hath no man than this, that a man lay down his life for his friends."

Also on the reverse side are the geographical outlines of the United States and Canada. Surrounding the inscription plate are sprigs of laurel for glory, ivy for friendship, oak for strength, and thistle for persistence.

Medals are of bronze, silver, and gold. More than 90 percent of the medals awarded to date have been bronze. Only a little over 600 have been silver. These have been awarded in cases involving prolonged or repeated risks.

For example, the awarding of a silver medal might be considered in a fire case in which a rescuer goes repeatedly through a wall of fire. In such a case, the risk is more visible; the danger is obvious.

Gold medals are the most rare. Only nineteen have been awarded. The last one was conferred in 1958, when a special award was given in honor of the heroes of a mine disaster at Springhill, Nova Scotia. A similar award was made in the case of the heroes of the *Titanic,* the great ocean liner that ran into a huge iceberg in the North Atlantic Ocean off the coast of Newfoundland on its maiden voyage in 1912.

Through the years, the commission has maintained a set of eligibility standards so rigid that only about one case of every ten considered receives an award.

The most demanding single qualification reads: "There must be conclusive evidence that the person performing the act voluntarily risked his [or her] own life to an extraordinary degree in saving or attempting to save the life of another person, or voluntarily sacrificed himself [or herself] in an heroic manner for the benefit of others."

The commission is made up of prominent business people and civic leaders. Reporting to them is a small staff of field investigators who travel all over the United States and Canada to check out reports of heroism. These reports come from a variety of sources: newspaper accounts, letters or calls from private citizens, civic officials, service organizations, and others.

Investigators do a thorough job, interviewing the rescuers and the victims, if they are still alive, in addition to eyewitnesses, newspaper reporters, and anyone else connected with a case. Then they file extensive reports with the commission for final evaluation.

The commission breaks heroism down into fourteen separate categories that cover just about everything imaginable. There are several classifications for drownings and fires. Others include rescues from paths of moving vehicles; from high elevations such as mountains, bridges, and buildings; from electric shock; from animal attacks; escapes from tanks and other chambers, and from caved-in tunnels; free-fall catch; and rescue from homicidal attack.

The types of rescues have changed through the years. "We don't get any rescues from the paths of horse-drawn wagons anymore," says commission secretary Walter Toerge. "Forty to fifty years ago we used to have a lot of runaway-horse situations, and cases of people who had fallen into hand-dug wells and cesspools. Today we're more likely to have a rescue in a remote area from a snowmobile accident, or a crashed and burning automobile."

Rescues from drowning annually account for between one third and one half of all award winners. Rescues from burning vehicles and from burning buildings are usually a close second. But the range varies greatly.

People have been rescued from attacks by grizzly bears, enraged bulls, mad dogs, cougars, and other wild animals. Others have been saved from high-voltage lines, fume-clogged tanks, caved-in tunnels, and the narrow ledges of steep mountain walls. Some have been rescued from homicidal attacks.

Rescues of people in danger thus come in virtually every conceivable form and location, including air crashes, sea disasters, and tragedies at home or on the highway.

3.

Characteristics of Courage

☐ A few years ago on a warm summer night, a young woman named Kitty Genovese was attacked by a man outside her apartment in Queens, a borough of New York City. She screamed and pleaded for help as the man stabbed her repeatedly with a knife. Dozens of people in neighboring apartments and in other places nearby heard her screams and saw what was happening. Yet no one came to her aid, and the attacker killed her and escaped from the scene.

Why did no one come forward to help her? Why, as Phil Williamson sat trapped in his flaming ice cream truck, did others stand by without moving while Bill Welch alone ran to Williamson's aid? Why, as Eugene Taylor sank to the bottom of a swimming pool, did others sit idly by while Karen Edwards, a thirteen-year-old girl, went to his rescue?

What makes a hero or heroine? Why is it that in a crowd of people seeing someone in danger, many times only one person will run forward to help save a life? How can one tell who has the quality of courage and who doesn't?

Experts at the Carnegie Hero Fund Commission do not know for sure. They say there is no known common

denominator to determine who will be a hero or heroine in a crisis situation and who won't.

"Psychologists tell us that only a certain percentage of people are capable of reacting positively under stress, but they don't know why," says Herbert Eyman, dean of the commission's investigators, now retired.

"Self-preservation is supposed to be the first law of nature, but our cases all involve something deeper than that. A person sees someone in trouble and just can't stand by and do nothing. It's a basic response. I think people act from deep-rooted instincts," Eyman says. "But there's no way you can say who has this quality and who doesn't."

Eyman recalls one case where a man was drowning in ocean surf so rough even professional lifeguards wouldn't enter it. They realized the hazards involved. Yet, mysteriously, a young girl who was a poor swimmer charged into the churning waves and saved the man's life.

"If you tried to explain such action by any selfish set of values, it would have to be considered foolhardy," Eyman says.

Commission files reveal only that heroes and heroines come from every age group, color, creed, and walk of life. They range from school-age youngsters to retired people. Carnegie medals have been awarded to boys and girls as young as eight years old, and to men and women in their seventies.

Some medal winners never realize the risks involved in a rescue attempt until long after it is over. Seventeen-year-old Craig Carrier of St. Louis, for instance, jumped repeatedly into foul-smelling liquid waste matter fifteen feet deep in a concrete-lined cesspool and brought up, alive, a two-year-old boy who had tumbled in and sunk to the bottom.

Only some time later did Craig fully understand the

hazards he faced. "All the time I was in the cesspool," he recalls, "I just kept telling myself I had to do it. But after it was over and I had time to think about it, I was scared to death."

Recalling his rescue of a baby in a runaway car, one teen-age student said things happened so fast he could barely remember what he did. He kept saying over and over, "I don't believe it." He also said that while he reacted on instinct, not everyone could do this.

Would these heroes and heroines risk their lives again in attempts to save others if they had it to do over? "I don't think they can answer that," Eyman says, "because the factors that moved them to action are so deep in their makeup."

Eyman believes there are probably millions of people who would make heroes and heroines, but who never come upon a situation to stir action. "The person who pauses to survey the situation probably will never get there," he says. "Most heroes seem to have no control over their actions. All their thoughts are centered on the plight of the person in trouble."

Commission experts say there are more heroes and heroines in their teens than there are in any other age group. And they cite some reasons for this.

"There is a higher percentage of young rescuers, especially teen-agers, because they are where the action is," says commission president Stewart McClintic. "They often are at the beach, boating, ice skating, and other places where accidents frequently happen.

"Also, boys and girls have faster reflexes than older people and can react quicker," says McClintic. "With kids, they see someone in trouble and they just can't stand by and do nothing."

But commission officials are quick to point out the hazards involved in attempting to save someone whose life is in danger.

"We stress safety above all else," says commission vice-president David Oliver. "Andrew Carnegie didn't want to encourage people into dangerous actions when he set up the fund." In fact, in creating the commission, Carnegie wrote: "Many thought that its purpose was to stimulate heroic action, that heroes were to be induced to play their parts for the sake of reward. This never entered my mind. True heroes think not of reward. They are inspired and think only of their fellows endangered; never of themselves."

In the commission's files are many cases through the years where boys and girls have lost their own lives while trying to save others, or have been seriously injured attempting a rescue.

Even teen-age medal winners advise others about the unsafety of their acts. One boy who saved a man from drowning in rough surf says, "If possible, I strongly suggest that anyone not attempt to perform the rescue on their own. If there are any other people in the area, give them a shout, because it is so easy to get caught in the same trap as the person you're trying to save if you are by yourself."

But the problem, as Oliver and others point out, is that, in the majority of their cases, young people act from instinct when they see someone in trouble. It is a spur-of-the-moment reaction, often without thinking of personal consequences.

"We know that some people, a certain small percentage, will react instinctively to save a human life, regardless of how dangerous the circumstances are," Oliver says. "We can only say that we certainly don't encourage young people, or anyone else, to enter hazardous situations."

What makes a hero or heroine? Who has this quality of courage and who doesn't, and why? Many studies have been made in an attempt to find out. And commission officials have reviewed thousands of cases of heroism over nearly three quarters of a century. But still no one really knows the answer.

4.

Danger in the Water

☐ It was one of Chicago's first "warm" days after a long, dreary winter. The temperature had actually gotten above freezing, to 35 degrees Fahrenheit. Nine-year-old Luther Tillman was having fun sliding along the ice that covered Sherman Park Lagoon. He apparently had not heard the message being broadcast over the park's public address system warning people to stay off the ice.

Suddenly the ice cracked under him, and Luther sank into the frigid waters. As he surfaced, he screamed for help. Leon Walker and John Hamilton, both seventeen, ran toward the lagoon, and Leon's sixteen-year-old brother, John, followed them.

While the others stayed on the bank, Leon walked hurriedly out on the ice toward Luther. What Leon didn't know was that the best way to reach such a person on thin ice is to crawl. This distributes a person's weight more evenly, reducing the chances of the ice giving way.

Leon got to within two feet of Luther and reached out his hand. Luther grabbed it, but, as Leon pulled him out, the ice broke and he, too, fell into the water. Luther climbed on his back, but Leon shook him off and told him to hold on to the edge of the ice. Leon then called to John Hamilton to help them.

Again the weakened ice collapsed, and Hamilton plunged into the water. All three boys struggled briefly, then yelled to John Walker for help.

"Be careful," Leon hollered to John as he approached the widening hole in the ice. John reached for Hamilton and tried to pull him out, but instead the ice cracked some more and he fell in. Now all four boys were in trouble.

At that instant, seventeen-year-old Victor Carl Edwards, a strapping boy of six foot one and 178 pounds, was riding on a bus passing the park.

"Someone's drowning in the lagoon," he shouted. "Stop the bus!"

The driver stopped and Victor raced toward the boys. While several others stood by on the bank, he walked out on the ice, dropping to his knees when he was about fifteen feet from the hole. He noticed that Hamilton and the Walker brothers appeared to be okay, holding on to the edge of the ice. But Luther seemed dazed.

"Hang on," he told Luther. "I'll get you out."

But as he got within two feet of Luther, the ice gave way and he fell into the water. Victor quickly used his long arms to pull himself up on the ice, then turned and reached Leon Walker and pulled him out, dragging him on his stomach to the east bank.

Leon raced into the street to hail a passing motorist to get help. As he did, Victor ran to a small tree at the edge of the lagoon and broke off a branch. Then he ran back to the hole, but only John Hamilton and John Walker could be seen. Luther had disappeared.

Victor crawled to within three feet of the hole and extended the branch to Hamilton, who grasped it and was pulled out of the water. A man on the bank then gave Victor a six-foot-long chain leash and he went back and pulled John Walker out with it.

After reaching the bank safely with John, Victor returned to the hole once again to look for Luther. And again he fell through the ice. He dived to the bottom of the murky lagoon, feeling with his arms for Luther, but couldn't locate him.

By this time police had arrived, and they threw a long rope to Victor and pulled him out of the water. Victor sat down on the bank and cried because he could not find Luther. Luther's body was brought up later by divers.

John Hamilton and Leon and John Walker all quickly recovered. Victor was taken to a hospital and treated for frostbite, exposure, and shock, and was released two days later.

Victor's courage was especially noteworthy because he realized his own life was in danger. Even after falling into the water, he went back three times to help the others. It was an outstanding individual act of heroism.

☐ Drowning rescues account each year for between one third and one half of the commission's awards. This is because so many accidents occur in the water: at beaches, where there are often strong undertows and currents; in boating accidents in deep water; in swimming pools where non-swimmers or poor swimmers get into water too deep; and on ice-covered ponds, lakes, and rivers.

Drowning rescues have also accounted for some of the commission's most dramatic case histories over the years. The files are full of extraordinary feats of courage involving water rescues. In some instances, boys and girls who couldn't swim at all have fearlessly dived into deep or rough waters in attempts to help people in trouble. Many young people have lost their lives while trying to save others from drowning.

In one such case in Kemptville, Ontario, Canada, ten-year-old Sheila Mackey waded out too deep in a swimming hole in the Rideau River. She swallowed some water, panicked, and screamed for help. A nine-year-old girl reached her, but, in her fear, Sheila forced the girl under water. When the girl surfaced, she swam away.

Thirteen-year-old Thomas Smart then came to Sheila's aid. He was tired, having just swum across the river and back, and when he reached her, Sheila grasped him by the shoulders from behind, and he went under water.

Near exhaustion and out of breath, Thomas, with a last burst of energy, shoved Sheila toward the shore. By this time a woman who had heard the children shouting had run to the river. She swam out, got to Sheila, and towed her to safety.

"Where's Thomas?" someone then asked. He was nowhere in sight. He was later found near the mud bottom of the river and was given mouth-to-mouth resuscitation, but could not be revived. He had sacrificed his life to save Sheila's.

☐ It was to be a fun outing, but it turned into a tragedy for twenty-six members of a boy scout troop in Dragerton, Utah. In rubber rafts bound together in a platform, they were fording down the Green River. Rounding a bend in the river, the rafts were swept up against a large tree that had become lodged against a boulder at midstream.

Several of the rafts capsized, and the boys were thrown into the swirling waters. The scout leaders and most of the boys climbed onto the tree and reached safety on the boulder. Six boys were missing, but then the leaders found four of them walking on the west bank.

Now only two were unaccounted for: fourteen-year-old Peter McCarthy and ten-year-old James Bernardoni. When he was thrown out of his raft, James got caught in the tree branches beneath the surface of the water. Keeping calm, he eased out of his life jacket by pulling it up over his head. When he surfaced, he saw Peter nearby, and Peter told him to hang on to his life jacket. As they began floating downstream, out of sight from the others, James became frightened.

"Don't panic," Peter kept saying. "We'll get out of this. Hang on."

The currents moved them swiftly down the river, and with the extra weight of the two boys for only one life jacket, they floated low in the river.

At times Peter and James were carried near one of the river's banks, but they were too exhausted to try to swim for it, and continued floating. After more than an hour in the water, they were swept over a five-foot water-fall, and both boys by this time had swallowed a lot of water. Still Peter kept reassuring James.

"We'll make it. Don't worry," he kept saying.

In two hours they floated five miles downstream. By this time Peter was still conscious, but James could no longer understand him. Then James noticed a fallen tree on the west bank with a limb extending into the water. He let go of Peter's life jacket and grabbed hold of the limb. Then, staggering from fatigue, he made his way to the shore.

When James last saw him, Peter was gasping for air, his lips were blue, and he was floating low in the water. James spent the night on the riverbank, then continued walking downstream the next morning. When he was picked up by some men in rafts, he was fifteen miles from where the accident had happened.

At about the same time, some boys fishing another fifteen miles down the river saw Peter floating face down in the water. He had drowned, probably not realizing that he had saved James's life.

5.

Floods and
Wind-whipped Waves

☐ Often accidents occur when they are least expected. One afternoon in the small town of Emo, Ontario, for example, three-year-old Wade McDonald was playing around his house. Unnoticed by his father, Wade climbed into the family car, a 1965 Studebaker four-door sedan, which was parked on the McDonalds' sloping driveway. He pretended, as small children sometimes do, to be driving the car, steering the wheel back and forth. Then, as he had often seen his father do, Wade released the car's emergency brake.

The car began rolling down the steep driveway, picking up speed as it crossed River Street. Totally out of control, it rolled over the bank of the Rainy River and plunged into the water. Just as it did, fifteen-year-old Francis Sheppard and a friend of his were walking up the street and saw what happened.

"Hey," Francis's friend shouted. "Someone's in that car!"

"I think you're right," Francis answered. As he ran to the riverbank, his friend raced toward the McDonald home. At the edge of the water, which was choppy and swollen and with a strong current from recent rains,

Francis could see Wade standing up in the front seat as the car floated westward from the bank.

With no one else in sight, Francis dived into the river without even taking the time to remove his boots. The water was a bone-chilling 42 degrees, but Francis, a good swimmer, made it to the car without any trouble. As he did, only the windows and roof of the Studebaker were still above water.

By this time Wade's father and a number of other people had gathered on the bank and were watching as Francis carefully worked his way around to the driver's side of the car, where the rear window was open. His teeth were chattering and his body was shaking from the cold water, and he could see that the back seat of the car was now filled with water.

Pushing his head through the open window, Francis tried to reach Wade, who was scared and still standing up in the front seat. But he couldn't quite reach him. Then, holding the bottom of the window frame with one hand, Francis wedged part of his body through the window and pulled Wade over the back of the front seat.

While water began gushing into the open window, Francis put his left arm under Wade's chin and started to pull him out of the car, but the frightened child held on tight to a rain gutter above the car's window as the car began to tilt sharply in the water. Francis had to brace both his feet against the car door and push back to break Wade's hold. Once free of the car, Francis paddled away on his back with Wade lying on his chest.

Extremely tired now, Francis stopped a second to rest, and saw the car disappear from sight and sink to the bottom of the river. Seeing how tired Francis was, Wade's father and another man dived into the water, swam to him, and helped the two boys back to the bank. Both recovered without any lasting ill effects.

☐ Violent, unpredictable weather often causes accidents. Four teen-age boys were fishing about two miles out in Mobile Bay in Alabama one April when a sudden squall hit, furiously churning up large waves and rocking their small craft as if it were a toy boat. The boys piloted the boat to a fixed buoy, tied it up to some pilings, and climbed a ladder to a wooden deck to wait out the storm.

The wind-whipped waves became three to four feet high, and the line on the boat snapped. It began drifting off to the southwest. Seventeen-year-old Donald Moody dived into the rough waters and began swimming after it. But after he had swum 120 feet, he still was 100 feet from the boat. Tired and winded, he turned and started back toward the buoy. But now the wind and the waves were in his face, and he swallowed a lot of water.

"I don't see him," cried sixteen-year-old Paul Wilson. "He went under and he didn't come up." Paul, who knew that neither of the other two boys was a good swimmer, dived into the water fully clothed and began swimming toward Donald. With the wind at his back, he had no trouble, and he found Donald submerged in the water about 190 feet from the buoy. He was unconscious. Paul tucked an arm under Donald's chin and began towing him against the wind and waves.

Suddenly Donald revived and, panicking, grasped Paul at the shoulders and neck and tried to climb onto him. The two boys struggled in the stormy waters and went under three times. Realizing now that both their lives were in danger, Paul hit Donald hard in the face with his fist, and Donald went limp.

Weakened by the struggle in the water, Paul again began towing Donald back toward the buoy, but it was slow going. Paul's arms and legs ached with fatigue, and he was heaving for breath. But he knew he had to reach the buoy or they would both drown. He trod water for a while, trying to catch his wind. Finally, after an exhausting effort, he managed to reach the pilings underneath the ladder and lunged forward with Donald. He grabbed hold of the pilings even though they were covered with sharp barnacles that cut into his arm.

The other two boys reached down and got hold of Donald. Then they went back down the ladder and helped Paul, who now was bleeding badly from the barnacle cuts. Donald had stopped breathing, but the boys gave him artificial respiration and he came to. The four of them huddled on the deck for twelve hours before a man in a motorboat picked them up. Donald recovered fully within a month, and Paul's cuts healed in about two weeks.

☐ The Carnegie Hero Fund Commission's files contain hundreds of dramatic rescues from water hazards. In some, people put forth almost superhuman efforts to save others from drowning. And in rare instances, several persons have been saved at one time. One such case occurred a few years ago on a rainy May evening on the Mohican River near the town of Brinkhaven, Ohio.

There were about one hundred children on the east bank of the river, all attending the summer camp of the city of Newark, Ohio. Heavy rains had caused the river to swell considerably, and after dinner one of the camp's teachers and about twelve children walked out on a suspension footbridge to watch the swift-moving water flow underneath.

Then, disaster. The weight of the group caused the bridge to sag into the water, and the rapid current quickly tore the bridge loose from its supports.

The screams of the children filled the air. Some of them clung to the wreckage, but several others were swept downstream.

Inside the camp dining hall, sixteen-year-old Ric Courson and nineteen-year-old Thomas Terry heard the screams, raced outside, and saw the children drifting helplessly in the raging water.

Five of the children, most of them ten to twelve years old, had been washed into a pile of floating driftwood about ten feet from the north end of an island in the middle of the river. Tree limbs and other debris had become matted together. Four of the boys and girls worked their way onto the driftwood, but the fifth child had become entangled under the debris and was not noticed by the others.

Meanwhile, six other children had caught hold of some bushes in the middle of the river's channel east of the island, where they huddled together, frightened and cold.

Ric and Thomas jumped into the water and began wading toward the children. Thomas then submerged in water over his head and for a moment was afraid he would be swept downstream, or would be caught in some of the heavy debris that was floating in the river. When he surfaced, he began swimming toward the island.

Ric also began swimming, and both boys reached the island a few minutes later, having drifted eighty feet downstream from where they had entered the water. Then they ran to the north end of the island and waded out to the clump of bushes which the children still were clinging on to.

Despite the strong current, they each reached a child at a time and carried them back to the island. After four children had been saved, twelve-year-old Diana Mason cried out.

"Help! I can't hold on any longer," she screamed as she lost her grip on the bushes and began floating downstream. She tried to swim, but the current was too strong.

Ric ran across the island and swam about twenty feet out, where he intercepted Diana, who grabbed hold of his outstretched hand. While he towed her back toward the island, his face tensed up as severe leg cramps hit his calves. Now he wasn't sure whether he could make it or not. He let the current carry them downstream about one hundred feet, where they reached wadable water. Then, holding on to bushes, they made it to the south end of the island.

While this was happening, Thomas had removed two other children from the clump of bushes. Next, Ric and Thomas ran to the four children who had been clinging on to the driftwood. The boys could see these children were tiring, and they knew they had to get to them fast before the current pulled them away.

But there was a ten-foot gap of deep water between the island and where the children were, and Ric and Thomas could see the current here was far too swift for them to get across.

They looked around and saw that a tree limb about fifteen feet long and four to eight inches thick had fallen across the gap. One end of the limb was lodged against one of the trees holding the driftwood. Thomas locked his arms around the limb to support it, while Ric waded across the swift-moving water, holding on to the limb. He then picked up one girl and waded back across the gap holding on to the limb with his free arm. He went back three more times and brought back the other three children.

Later, one girl was found drowned, her body wedged underwater in the debris. But eleven other children were alive.

6.

Flaming Inferno

□ It takes a special kind of courage to enter a building that is on fire, or to race toward a flaming vehicle whose gas tank could explode at any second. Fire can be terrifying, and many people die annually from burns and smoke inhalation because no one would dare come to their rescue.

However, in the Carnegie Hero Fund Commission's files are many cases where people unselfishly risked their lives, or took the chance of being badly burned and scarred for life, by braving raging flames and intense heat in attempts to save others. Many of these heroes and heroines have been young people.

□ Three small children, one-year-old Michel Lachapelle, his four-year-old sister, and his two-year-old brother, had been put to bed in two of the three bedrooms in the finished basement of their home in Montreal, Canada, by three baby-sitters, while the parents had gone out for the evening. The three girls caring for the children were upstairs on the main floor of the building.

While Michel slept in his crib, the other two children apparently had been playing with a blanket and left it over an electric heater. The blanket smoldered for several minutes, then, at about 8 P.M., it burst into flames, and fire broke out in the basement.

The children began screaming, and one of the baby-sitters ran to the basement staircase. Flames were shooting up the stairs, so she ran out of the house, across the street to the home of sixteen-year-old high school student Gerald Doherty. Gerald, his father, and a fifteen-year-old friend then ran to the Lachapelle home. They couldn't get in the front door, because when the other two baby-sitters had run out the door, it had automatically locked behind them.

Gerald and the others then went around to the basement windows, which were covered on the outside by heavy wire grating. Gerald peered inside and saw smoke already entering the bedrooms and flames shooting up in the hallway beyond. Some men who had arrived at the scene removed the grating and kicked in the glass of one of the basement windows.

Gerald picked large pieces of glass out of the frame and then saw, inside, Michel's brother and sister together on a bed in one of the bedrooms.

"Come over here, quick," he called to them. "Come here and I'll get you out."

But the children were horror-stricken and did not move. So Gerald crawled in through the window, which was about five feet above the floor level inside, and dropped to the floor. He ran through dense swirls of smoke to the two children, scooped them up from their bed, and took them back to the window. He passed each child through the opening to men outside. Gerald was now coughing badly from the smoke and was about to climb outside himself when one of the baby-sitters screamed at him.

"Get Michel!" she yelled. "He's in the back bedroom."

Gerald went back through one bedroom and into the hall, where leaping flames stretched from the floor to the ceiling. Shielding his face with one hand, Gerald crouched against one wall and ran past the flames to another bedroom, choking and coughing from breathing in the smoke. He opened the door, but in the dark he could see nothing.

"Are you in here, Michel?" he called out. He heard nothing. By now the flames, heat, and smoke had increased, and he had started to head back to the open basement window when he noticed the partly open door to the third bedroom. He pushed the door open and, by the light of the flames in the hall, saw Michel in his crib. He picked him up and re-entered the fiery hall. Now Gerald was coughing violently.

He thought for an instant that he might wait in Michel's bedroom in the hope that someone outside would open its window. Then he was afraid if they didn't open it in the next minute or two, he might be trapped. So he decided to head back down the hall to the open window at the other end. But now flames had enveloped the whole hallway, turning it into a roaring inferno.

Coughing uncontrollably, Gerald held Michel close to his chest and dashed sideways through the hall. He got past the worst flames, but still was in blinding smoke, when one of his shoes came off and he tripped and fell, losing his hold on the child. Quickly he got to his feet, picked Michel up, and made it to the bedroom where the open window was. The room was filled with smoke. He fell again, but struggled to his feet and made it to the window. He handed Michel to people outside.

Overcome and blinded by the smoke, and breathless, Gerald felt he might collapse. But somehow he grasped the windowsill, and his father and others outside grabbed his arms and pulled him out of the room. Michel and the other children were fine, and Gerald was treated at a hospital for first-degree burns on his arms and nose and then released.

☐ Likewise, four people in California are alive and well today thanks to young Kevin Coulter of Canoga Park, near Los Angeles, who risked his life, not once, but four different times in a valiant act of heroism.

Kevin was eighteen at the time, and his car had broken down early in the morning on the southbound San Diego Freeway, one of the busiest highways in the country. He had pulled over and stopped on the paved shoulder.

A light rain was falling as Mrs. Paula Ramsey drove her 1971 Dodge Colt south on the freeway. With her in the car were her husband, James, and, in the rear seat, Harold Young and Jeanette Luhr.

Without warning, Mrs. Ramsey lost control of the car on the rain-slick road and it began sliding out of control at about sixty miles per hour. She skidded across several lanes of traffic and smashed into a four-foot concrete retaining wall that separated the north- and southbound lanes of the highway.

Careening against the wall, the Dodge then smacked into Kevin's parked car, injuring him slightly. The impact flipped the Dodge over onto its roof, where it finally stopped in the middle of the freeway.

All four people in the Dodge, none of whom had been wearing a seat belt, were injured and unconscious. A small fire erupted on the underside of the car near the engine, sending out tongues of flame a foot high.

Others drivers, seeing the accident, stopped on the road shoulder and watched the fire. Kevin was still in his car, and his back hurt from the jarring collision, but he was afraid the Dodge might explode and kill the people inside, so he ran to the driver's side of the car, stooped down, and looked inside.

The two men were sprawled on the roof of the car as it lay upside down, and the two women were on top of them. Another man ran up to Kevin.

"Let's jerk them out of there fast, before the gas tank explodes," he yelled.

"No," Kevin shouted back. "They may be badly hurt, and if we aren't careful in moving them, they could be seriously injured."

The man then hurried away, leaving Kevin alone. He reached through the open window on the driver's side, grabbed Mrs. Ramsey under her armpits, and pulled her out of the car. He then carried her about thirty feet away and laid her down. He went back to the car and, working gently and carefully, removed Mr. Ramsey and set him down beside his wife.

Back again he went to the car, as others stood by and just watched. But now the fire had broken out over the entire front half of the Dodge, and the flames were two feet high. Kevin wiped the sweat from his forehead with the back of his hand and kneeled down to the window. He drew Miss Luhr out of the car and carried her a safe distance away. By this time a small crowd of passing motorists had stopped to watch, but still no one volunteered to come forward and help.

Tired, hot, and afraid of the fast-spreading flames, Kevin ran back to the Dodge a fourth time, kneeled down, and tried to pull Young from the car, but he couldn't budge him. Kevin noticed that a suitcase and the cushion of the rear seat were lying on top of Young, so he crawled inside the car, despite the heat and flames, moved the obstacles away, and then dragged Young out.

No sooner had he laid Young down beside the others than the fire reached the Dodge's full fuel tank and there was an explosive swoosh as the gas-fed flames engulfed the car.

The Ramseys, Miss Luhr, and Young all recovered from their injuries and suffered no burns.

7.

Explosive Situations

☐ In addition to fear of the danger of being burned by fire or suffocating from smoke, many people will not go near a flaming building or vehicle for fear of an explosion. Gas tanks, gas or oil heaters and pipelines, among other things, could trigger such an explosion at any point in a fire. And sometimes one explosion can set off a chain reaction of others, demolishing a building or a car or truck. To attempt to rescue someone in the face of such a terrible threat calls for a rare demonstration of courage.

It happened one December day in New York City. Nathaniel Weiss was in Irving Branzburg's print shop to get a printing job done when a violent blast ripped through the building, knocking both men to the floor. So devastating was the explosion, it caused the second floor of the building to collapse onto the first floor where they were.

Glass, wood, plaster, and concrete were thrown everywhere, pinning Weiss and Branzburg under two feet of rubble. Branzburg lay moaning, badly dazed. Weiss was conscious, but he was pinned under the debris. He couldn't move, and his leg was severely gashed and bleeding. Fire broke out in the back of the building. Live electrical wires dangled dangerously everywhere, and severed beams and jagged pieces of glass lay exposed.

Nineteen-year-old Larry Jackson, who had been across the street, ran to the scene. He saw the trapped men inside and, without thought of his own safety, went in after them. Larry and another man then lifted Branzburg up and carried him to the front of the print shop, where others helped him out into the street. They then went back to help Weiss.

"My leg," Weiss cried. "Please be careful. I think it's broken."

As he feverishly dug through the debris, Larry looked up and felt a cold stab of fear knife through him. Directly over his head, swaying dangerously, was a heavy steel beam. Should it break loose and drop, it could crush him. And all around him were the loose electrical wires. Flames also had begun eating at overhead timbers.

"Get out of there," a security guard yelled to Larry and the other man helping him. "This building's going to go up any minute. You'll all be killed!"

Despite his fears, Larry continued to dig, but he wasn't getting anywhere. The timbers and plaster were too heavy, and he knew time was running short. Larry and the other man got up and started walking about, looking for something that would help them pry off the heavy rubble that was holding Weiss. Larry walked out into the street, still looking. About fifteen seconds later a second explosion rocked the building, and giant flames immediately covered the entire first floor.

Larry sat down outside and began sobbing because he had not been able to free Weiss. Then he looked up and saw Weiss stumbling out of the fiery building. The second blast had somehow freed him, and, with help, he had managed to escape.

Ten people were killed in the explosions and the fire they set off. But Nathaniel Weiss and Irving Branzburg lived, thanks in large part to the heroic actions of teenager Larry Jackson.

☐ Sometimes an act of heroism cannot be directly measured in the number of lives saved. In one such case, it could have been several lives in addition to perhaps hundreds of thousands, or maybe even millions, of dollars that were spared because of the quick thinking of four young brothers who unselfishly risked their lives in a bizarre incident.

It happened a few years ago near the town of Titusville, Florida, not far from the famous Kennedy Space Center where moon rockets and other spacecraft are launched.

There had been a long and bitter strike by workers of the Florida East Coast Railroad. There had been much violence. Some men working for the railroad had been beaten up and their cars and homes had been damaged. Trains had been sabotaged. And with no end of the strike in sight, officials of the railroad feared more danger. So they often sent small scout cars ahead of trains to make sure the tracks had not been tampered with.

It was near dusk one evening when the four boys— Ander Hopkins, fourteen, and his brothers, Roger, eighteen, Delmar, twelve, and William, nine—were walking along the railroad tracks near the small community of Mims, just north of Titusville. They were on their way home after fishing.

They had noticed that a scout car had just passed, heading north, so they knew a freight train would be following soon. As they walked casually along the tracks,

Roger playfully pushed Ander, and his shoe got hooked beneath a wire.

"Hey, you guys, come here," Ander called. "Look what I found." Ander pulled on the wire and uncovered a small battery.

"What do you think it is?" he asked. The brothers gathered around him. Ander followed the wire, digging up dirt and gravel that covered it. He found something he first thought was a railroad flare. It was eighteen inches long and an inch and a half in diameter. Then he found another one. This one had the word *dynamite* marked on it.

"Look!" he shouted excitedly. "It's dynamite! Someone's trying to blow up the train. Help me dig. I think there's more here. We'd better get them out before the train comes."

Ander started digging frantically in the debris and found several more sticks of dynamite. Roger ran up and helped him, and he uncovered a detonator. He picked it out of the dirt and removed the wires from its terminals, broke it in two pieces, and tossed it aside.

In the next few minutes the four brothers dug up forty-five sticks of dynamite. One of them, wedged tightly beneath the tie, broke in half when they tried to remove it.

The boys made several trips, carrying the dynamite, battery, wires, and some coat hangers that were attached, to a point about forty feet away from the tracks. As they were carefully moving the last few sticks, they heard a train whistle. The freight train was approaching.

Roger ran up the tracks and tried to flag down the train, but in the darkness the engine crew did not see him. The train passed at a speed of sixty miles per hour and the boys ran to safety, but no explosion occurred.

The Hopkins brothers then put everything they had found in a box and started home. But it was so heavy to carry, they hid it in a culvert and ran home and told their father. He called the sheriff, and officers later removed the half stick of dynamite that had broken off and another whole one.

The boys learned afterward that the dynamite—each stick containing 40 percent nitroglycerin—had been rigged so that the coat hangers would make contact with tie plates when the train passed. This would close an electrical circuit, activate the detonator, and set off the dynamite.

Ander spoke for his brothers when he said he was scared the minute he saw the word *dynamite* on one of the sticks. The boys were afraid they could have gone off even without an electrical detonation.

But had it not been for the brothers' cool thinking and quick work, risking their lives, the forty-seven sticks of dynamite would have blown the train to pieces and probably killed the entire crew.

8.

Hazards of High Voltage

☐ Heavy summer rains had pelted the area around Charleston, West Virginia, for days, and the rivers had swollen and spilled over their banks, flooding the countryside. On a Sunday evening in July, fifteen-year-old David Carney, his parents, and David's friend Joseph Long, Jr., drove out to Sissonville to view the damage created by the rampaging Tuppers Creek.

David and Joseph got out of the car to take some pictures. They waded knee deep in the water as they walked north on the road. But after a few minutes their clothing got wet, and they realized the water overflowing from the creek was still rising, so they started back toward higher ground.

With David in front, they entered the yard of a house west of the road and saw what looked like a clothesline. Actually it was a temporary power line consisting of two uninsulated copper wires carrying 110 volts of alternating current. The wires, which were thirty inches apart, extended about forty feet from a shed to a post.

As they walked across the lawn, David slipped on the wet grass, and, trying to keep from falling, instinctively reached out and grabbed one of the wires.

A jolt of electricity surged through him, convulsing

☐ 46

his body as he clutched the wire with both hands. He slumped forward, unconscious. Because his feet and part of his body were still in contact with the wet grass, charges of electricity continued to course through him.

Joseph saw David fall and thought he had hurt himself. He walked over to him and put his hand on David's back. Joseph jumped back when he received a strong electrical shock.

"Help!" Joseph shouted. "Somebody please help! My friend's being electrocuted." But David's parents, in the car, were too far away to hear. Joseph, who held Red Cross certificates in both water rescue and first aid, including some training in dealing with electric shock, was afraid David might be killed if he didn't act fast. He fully realized his own danger.

He stooped down and grabbed David by the ankles in an effort to try and pull him free of the wire, but he again received a strong electrical shock, which knocked his hands free.

Joseph then looked around him and saw a water-soaked piece of wood about two feet long lying nearby. He picked it up and extended it to David's wrist, again trying to loosen his grasp on the wire, but once more he shivered when another severe electrical jolt ran through him, and he dropped the wood.

"Help! My friend needs help. Somebody, anybody," Joseph continued to shout as he looked about for some other rescue aid.

Hearing the shouts, eighteen-year-old Thomas Henshaw ran out of the house next door and saw David draped over the wire.

Thomas then grabbed hold of the wire and jerked it toward himself, as if trying to shake David free. One of David's hands came loose, but then Thomas slumped forward over the wire. Joseph once more grabbed David by the ankles. This time the shock was not as strong and he pulled hard. David's other hand came loose and he fell to the ground.

Joseph dropped to his knees and began mouth-to-mouth resuscitation. Come on, David, Joseph thought to himself as he worked over him. Come on, breathe. After two minutes, David responded, catching his breath and moaning low.

Joseph then got up and turned his attention to Thomas, who was still holding the wire with both hands while his bare chest rested on it. David's father arrived and picked up a stick, striking the wire repeatedly, trying to jar Thomas loose, but he couldn't.

Then he found an ax and smashed the electric meter attached to the outside of the house. This, at last, halted the flow of electricity, and Thomas fell free of the wire. He had been draped on it for about seven minutes.

Joseph then tried mouth-to-mouth resuscitation on Thomas, and later firemen arrived and administered oxygen, but he could not be revived. David Carney, who had held the wire for about three minutes, received slight burns on his hands, but recovered fully.

For their continued courageous efforts, both Joseph Long and Thomas Henshaw were awarded bronze Carnegie hero medals. Henshaw's was presented to his parents, posthumously.

☐ It was chilly for a baseball game, 60 degrees, when the two high school teams began play in Lucedale, Mississippi. There were only about forty fans in the bleachers, mostly parents of the players.

Sixteen-year-old Mark McLendon, relaxing between innings, was standing at an open gate of chain-link fencing. His left arm was extended on top of the gate and his right hand rested on the gatepost. Unknown to him or anyone else at the field, an uninsulated guy wire, stretched from the top of a utility pole, lay on the fence.

It was late March, and at 5:30 P.M., with cloudy, overcast skies, it was getting dark.

"Turn on the lights," the home-plate umpire called out. A coach walked down to the switchbox and flipped the power switch on.

At that instant, several thousand volts of electricity surged from a utility pole to the uninsulated power lines to the loose guy wire and to the fence. Immediately the power flow pulsed through Mark's body, because, by holding on to the gate and the fence, he was in effect providing a connecting link between sections of the fence.

Sparks shot out of his left hand and there was a ball of fire in his palm. Mark's head was thrown backward and his eyes rolled back. He was jolted unconscious almost instantaneously.

Standing a few feet away from Mark was seventeen-year-old Davis Sellers, a teammate. Afraid that Mark might be killed by the voltage, and scared that he might also be electrocuted if he touched Mark, Davis first thought of knocking Mark free of his grip on the fence with a baseball bat.

But worried that such action might take too long, he ran toward Mark and leaped in the air, striking him with his right arm and shoulder while his feet were off the ground. The blow knocked Mark backward, breaking his contact with the fence.

Davis felt a "tingling sensation in his feet" when he landed, but kept his balance and grabbed hold of Mark, as the coach turned the electrical switch off.

Several men ran to the boys, and shortly after mouth-

to-mouth resuscitation was begun, Mark began normal breathing. He was hospitalized for two weeks for first- and second-degree burns on his right hand and third-degree burns on his left arm, but he recovered with no lasting ill effects.

Davis was a little shaken up, but not hurt. His remarkable quick thinking not only spared him from possible serious injury, but probably saved Mark McLendon's life.

9.

Watch Out for the Train!

☐ Nearly all life-saving rescues call for fast action. When people are drowning or trapped in fiery buildings or cars, there is little time to think. Responses must be quick and positive if lives are to be spared. But of all the rescue categories, none requires more split-second timing than those involving saving someone from the path of a speeding train, truck, or car.

Fourteen-year-old Ronald Barreras was horseback riding with three teen-age girls and two twelve-year-old boys near Pico Rivera, California. One of the girls, Hope Alvarado, had ridden only once before and that had been a year ago.

About a mile from the stables, they approached a railroad track crossing. A large mound of earth, supporting a bridge just south of the track, prevented them from seeing a forty-seven-car freight train speeding toward them. The two boys and one of the girls crossed the tracks just as the fast-approaching train, now 800 feet away, sounded its whistle.

"Watch out, there's a train coming," one of the girls yelled. But she didn't say from which direction. Meanwhile, Hope Alvarado's horse had stopped right at the track's edge.

"Gettie up," she screamed at the horse, but it wouldn't move. It was apparently frightened by the train whistle. Desperate, she yanked on the animal's reins, but it still wouldn't budge. The train bore down on them.

Hope screamed hysterically as the train's engineer, seeing her, applied his emergency brakes. But he knew he wouldn't be able to stop in time.

Hearing the train's screeching brakes, and seeing that Hope was in trouble, Ronald urged his horse forward. He rode up next to Hope's horse and struck it with a whip. It did not move. Seeing the train only a short distance away, and realizing that there wasn't a second to spare, Ronald inched his horse forward and took hold of the reins held by Hope. By pulling hard on the horse's bit, he moved it away from the track. However, his own horse now was within a foot of the north rail. As the train reached them, Hope managed to move her horse free and rode away.

But the train's engine struck Ronald's horse in the rear, killing it, and severed Ronald's left leg at the calf, knocking him hard to the ground, where he lost consciousness. The train finally stopped 1,800 feet down the track. Hope, seeing Ronald lying on the ground, rode for help. An ambulance arrived twenty minutes later and rushed him to the hospital after members of the train crew had administered first aid to stop the bleeding.

In addition to the loss of his leg, Ronald Barreras suffered a fractured skull, a dislocated right collarbone, and lacerations of his right leg. But within a month he had recuperated, and later was awarded a bronze medal by the Carnegie Hero Fund Commission for his courageous action, which had saved Hope Alvarado's life.

☐ Shortly after 3 P.M. on a bright October after-

☐ *53*

noon, sixteen-year-old John Minadeo took up his position on a corner of Second Avenue near the Gladstone Elementary and Junior High School in Pittsburgh, Pennsylvania. Only two weeks before he had been appointed captain of the school safety patrol after three years of service.

His job was to keep students safely on the sidewalk until the light at the busy intersection turned green and the traffic had cleared. At 3:05 P.M., school was dismissed and the 1,200 students began walking home.

At that instant, a man in a car driving southeast down a steep hill on Hazelwood Avenue pressed on his brake pedal to slow down, but nothing happened. The brakes failed, and his car picked up speed rapidly.

A woman police guard a block above where John was stationed saw the runaway car approaching, and she quickly herded a group of children back onto the curb. Then she began blowing her whistle to warn others, as the car careened past her going more than fifty miles per hour, heading toward the Second Avenue intersection.

The car narrowly missed another vehicle, grazed a fire alarm box and utility pole, and swerved west, its right wheels mounting the curb, heading straight toward John and several girls who were standing there waiting for the light to change.

Seeing the onrushing car, John did not panic or run. Instead, he held both his arms outstretched in an effort to protect the girls. Just as he did, however, the right-side front of the car struck him directly, and the right front fender and bumper hit two of the girls and brushed past three others, knocking them to the sidewalk.

Still veering wildly out of control, the car carried John and the two girls on its front end until it ran over the curb at the west side of Second Avenue. John and one of the girls were then hurled to the pavement. Then the car struck a traffic light standard, throwing the other girl to the ground. The impact finally stopped the badly wrecked vehicle.

John and one of the girls were killed almost instantly and the other girl was knocked unconscious. The driver also was knocked out and suffered painful injuries.

But largely because of John Minadeo's heroic action in the face of death, three girls received relatively minor injuries, and the four girls recovered.

In addition to the medal awarded to John posthumously, a school in Pittsburgh was named after him.

☐ In the Bronx, New York, sixteen-year-old James Esteve Ribas and one of his high school buddies were waiting to board a subway train home one afternoon. Suddenly, to James's horror, his classmate slipped from the platform, struck his head on a rail, and lay helplessly sprawled across the track, just as a train approached.

While others stood by, shocked, James instinctively leaped down from the platform onto the tracks, jumped across an electrified rail, and reached the dazed youth. Again avoiding the electrified rail, he rolled him over, beneath the platform overhang, then tried to climb back up onto the platform as the train, unable to stop, bore down on them.

With jarring impact, the train struck James, dragging him twenty-five feet down the track along the edge of the platform, and clipped the heel of the other boy. Miraculously, James suffered only a severely bruised shoulder, and both boys soon recovered from their injuries.

☐ Disaster or near disaster can strike on an instant's notice, sometimes in the most unlikely places. Two-year-old Victor Scott was riding with his father in their

1970 Pontiac LeMans, when they stopped at a service station in Mount Holly, New Jersey.

The father put the car's transmission in park position and got out and walked toward the station building. Victor, standing on the front seat, moved over behind the wheel and pretended he was driving the car. He reached down, as he had often seen his father do, and shifted the automatic transmission gear selector into drive. The car began rolling down from the station apron toward a busy divided highway.

"Victor, no!" his father shouted, seeing the car picking up speed with his son behind the wheel. He began running after it.

Hearing the father shout, eighteen-year-old Gene John Miller, a college freshman working at the station part-time, quickly sized up the situation and also began chasing the car.

Victor's father caught up with the Pontiac, which was moving about fifteen miles per hour, just as it entered the street. He grabbed on to the right-side door handle, but couldn't open the door. Just then the car came within a foot of hitting two parked cars, squeezing Victor's father between them, and he lost his grip on the door.

Gene, meanwhile, kept racing after the car. He dashed out onto the highway without looking, but luckily there was no traffic. A track star in high school, he caught up with the car as it reached the northbound lanes of the highway bypass.

Reaching out as far as he could, Gene grasped the right door handle with his right hand, but he was running so fast, he couldn't open it. The car then jumped over a median curb. Gene tripped on the curb and fell to the ground, but rolled over and got to his feet quickly and continued chasing the car. Now it swerved over the median and headed northwest across the southbound lanes of the bypass road.

Again Gene ran across the road without even thinking of looking for oncoming traffic. His only thought was to reach the car and try to stop it before it crashed and injured or killed young Victor.

The car had left the road and was traveling through an asphalt parking lot next to a motel when Gene caught up with it once more. He grabbed the door handle on the driver's side with both hands and was dragged about forty feet, with his body fully extended, before he could manage to open the door.

Gene looked ahead and felt fear course through his body. The car was heading straight toward the motel building. He placed his right hand at the rear corner of the door sill and put his left hand on the top of the open door. He then swung his body forward, vaulting his legs into the car over the front seat. He slammed his right foot down hard on the brake pedal, jerking the car to an abrupt stop.

Victor, who had moved to the back seat, was thrown forward to the front seat, and Gene managed to catch him, even though the upper part of his body was still outside the car.

Victor's father and several others then reached the car. Victor and Gene were unhurt. Police later said the Pontiac had traveled nearly 400 feet before Gene stopped it. And he wasn't a second too soon. A scant 12 feet more, and it would have smashed into the motel's brick wall.

10.

Trapped in Wild Cat Cave

☐ With most rescues, it's almost a reflex action. It is instinctive. If someone's life is to be saved, the action must be virtually instantaneous. Once in a great while, however, an occasion will arise where a young person will have plenty of time to thoroughly assess and understand the dangers involved. When a teen-ager fully realizes his or her life is being risked in an effort to save another, it indeed becomes a courageous act of the highest order.

A classic example of this occurred a few years ago when a group of boys and girls from a children's home were on an outing at the Hinckley Reservation, part of the Cleveland, Ohio, metropolitan parks system.

To the youngsters, the most fascinating feature of the area was Wild Cat Cave. Legend held that runaway slaves had hidden out in the cave's darkest recesses before the Civil War. Fifteen-year-old Morris Baetzold, a slender teen, five feet eight inches tall, who weighed only 110 pounds, and two of his buddies were having fun exploring the cave, letting their imaginations run to extremes in the inky blackness.

After a few minutes, however, the boys were ready to leave. Morris's two friends went out of the cave entrance, but he lingered behind. He examined a huge slab of stone.

On one side of it was a narrow passage, no more than fifteen inches wide. It led down to the cave's floor. Intrigued, he decided to see if he could squeeze through the passage. The other boys had taken the flashlight, but Morris wasn't scared of the dark or the cold. It was 55 degrees in the cave.

A sense of excitement, unique to the explorer, rippled through Morris as he inched his way farther along the clammy stone walls. But then he slipped and his body wedged tightly in a crack about four and a half feet high, eighteen inches wide at the top and only nine inches wide at the bottom. His right arm was pinned beneath him. He scratched at the wall with his free left hand, but couldn't get a good hold.

Morris couldn't move one way or the other. The thrill of his exploration turned to fright and he began screaming for help. Outside, as the teachers boarded the children onto the school bus, they took a head count and came up one short.

"Morris is missing," someone said. Then everyone fanned out to look for him. When they returned to the cave, they heard Morris.

"Don't worry," one of the teachers shouted back. "We'll get you out of there." One of the boys ran to the nearest road, a quarter of a mile away, and flagged down a park ranger. In a short time the alarm had been passed on to local police and volunteer firemen, and they arrived at the scene with others.

One of the adults entered the cave and squirmed as far as he could into the fissure that was pinning Morris. But he couldn't get far enough to reach him. The firemen did manage to push a hose toward the boy, to send down oxygen and make breathing easier.

"Hold on," they kept reassuring Morris. "We'll get you out. It's only a matter of time."

Time now to Morris seemed an eternity. Word of his plight was picked up by the news media, and by late afternoon a large curious crowd had gathered. Morris had been trapped for six hours.

Morris's father and his eighteen-year-old brother were brought through the crowd to the cave. Inside, the rescue attempts were still going on. A slender fireman stretched far enough down the passage to throw a lasso over Morris's left leg. But as others pulled on the rope, Morris didn't move.

It became dark outside and a portable power generator was set up to illuminate the cave entrance. Radio and television news people broadcast continuing reports on what was happening.

Another rope was thrown to Morris, and he grabbed it with his left hand. But when this was pulled, he had no strength left to hold on. Firemen next reached down with a steel hook on a long pole. Morris caught the hook and put it in the collar of his jacket. When rescuers pulled on a rope attached to the hook, Morris moved slightly, but then the jacket tore and the hook ripped free.

Morris began crying. He was afraid now that they would never get him out of there; that he would die pinned tight against the walls of the passage.

Through the night the rescuers continued to think of a way to save the boy. A Cleveland mining company was called, and began preparing to bring up a drilling rig that could cut a shaft twenty-five feet down from the top of the cave's ledges. A trained cave rescue team from the National Speleological Society in Washington was flown in by special jet with an assortment of ropes, straps, and clamps. But even they were stumped, because no one was small enough or skinny enough to get close enough to Morris to hook him up.

A nurse volunteered to help. She was just five feet

two and weighed eighty-five pounds. She struggled to within a couple of feet of Morris, but then she panicked in the tight, clammy passageway and had to be pulled back.

At this point the professional rescuers were totally frustrated. They had some of the best experts in the country, and certainly the best equipment available, but it seemed they could do nothing. Dozens of ideas were discussed, but were discarded as being too impractical or too dangerous. The night passed.

Unknown to Morris or the rescuers, help was on the way from a completely unexpected source. Andrew Ulrich, a worker at an automotive plant who lived near Cleveland, was surprised to learn the next morning that Morris was still trapped. He had an idea. Maybe his sons, Michael, fifteen, and Gerald, twelve, could help. Both were small, wiry, and strong for their ages.

He called the plant and told his boss he wouldn't be at work that day. Then he and the boys headed for the cave. Officials were afraid of using inexperienced youngsters in such a dangerous situation, but Ulrich finally convinced them his sons might be able to get close enough to Morris to do some good.

Ropes and straps were tied around Gerald's chest and waist. He was four feet eleven and weighed eighty-two pounds, and he crept slowly, carefully, into the thin crack. He got to within six inches of Morris's foot, but then he got scared. He couldn't force himself to lean down. Choking for air, and nauseated, Gerald had to be pulled back out of the passage. He had come so close.

Determined, Andy Ulrich urged the rescuers to give Michael a chance. Ropes and straps were tied to him, and he put a nylon strap with a metal clamp into his left pants pocket. Then he began inching his way into the dark fissure. Ever so slowly, he lowered himself, head first, toward

Morris. It took him ten minutes to move eight feet. But eventually he worked himself close enough to touch Morris.

"Don't worry," Michael whispered. "We're going to get you out." Michael pulled the nylon strap out of his pocket and fastened it around Morris's left leg, just above the knee. Then he slipped the strap through the buckle and tightened it. He knotted a rope through the strap, using only his left hand, because he was using his right hand to support himself as he hung upside down above Morris. Despite the coolness of the cave, sweat rolled down Michael's forehead.

His work done, Michael slowly backed his way out of the fissure. The men above patted him on the back when he got out, praising him for the difficult job he had done. Then they pulled on the rope. Morris moved about two inches, but that was all. They were pulling him, but they weren't lifting him. If they continued to pull straight, they were afraid they would wedge Morris even tighter against the cave walls. They somehow had to find a way to raise the boy.

Exhausted from his ordeal, his arms cramped, Michael rested for several minutes, then volunteered to go back down to Morris. Again he inched his way down and reached him. This time he circled the strap around both of Morris's legs. Michael then felt along the rock wall, searching for something above Morris that would give the men the elevation they needed to lift him.

He found a small outcropping. Using his left hand and his teeth, Michael worked the strap's end into a loop around the projecting rock. This, he hoped, would act as a pulley, providing a force that would allow the men to pull Morris straight up and free him.

It took Michael another ten minutes to climb back

out. The men pulled again, easily, steadily. The tension was tremendous. If this didn't work, what else could they do?

But then they heard a shout from the darkness. "It's working," Morris yelled. "It's working." His hips had been raised from the wedge or rock, and he was able to free his right arm from under his body. His legs swung free, and were raised.

But the elation of everyone suddenly turned to dismay. Morris's chest was still stuck tight. They couldn't move him anymore.

Incredibly, Michael Ulrich, after another few minutes of rest, started down into the confined passageway for a third time. Again, using his left hand and teeth, he made a slip loop in a second long rope and pushed it across Morris's left hand and head. Morris then swung his right arm up through the loop and worked it down across his chest. Michael moved the other rope from Morris's legs and applied it at the shoulders.

When he crawled back this time to the mouth of the passage, Michael collapsed in fatigue. The rescuers then dumped a gallon of slippery glycerin down through a hose over Morris and shoved a narrow greased board under him.

Then they pulled on the ropes once more. Morris moaned as his chest and back scraped against the rough rocky ledge, but he was moving! His chest was freed.

Minutes later, after being trapped in the black pit for twenty-six and a half hours, Morris Baetzold was out of his rocky prison and alive; bruised, cramped, skinned, cold, afraid, and hungry, but alive!

11.

Gang Attacks and Guns

☐ There are, of course, many kinds of courage. It takes a certain kind, for example, for a person who is a poor swimmer, or who can't swim, to jump into deep or rough waters in an attempt to save someone who is drowning. It takes another kind to enter a flaming building. And, as most young people know, it even takes a special kind of courage to face up to a bully: someone who is bigger and tougher than they are. But to confront a whole gang of bullies, armed with knives, sticks, and other weapons, all by yourself, calls for an extraordinary display of courage.

Such was the situation that faced Pham Dang Duoc, a teen-age native of South Vietnam who was going to school in Washington, D.C. Pham's father worked in Washington at the South Vietnamese Embassy.

Pham was at a school dance one April evening with a friend, eighteen-year-old Robert Hennessee, when trouble broke out. Hennessee and another youth got into an argument. The teen-ager then struck Hennessee, who fought back, hitting and knocking down the boy.

A crowd gathered and a group of other youths started toward Hennessee, uttering threats.

"We're going to get you," one of them said.

"You're going to pay for what you've done," another muttered, as they closed in on him.

Scared, Hennessee ran out the south door of the dance hall and into the darkened parking lot. He was trying to reach his car and drive off, but about twenty to twenty-five in the gang ran close after him.

Pham, seeing what was happening, told someone to call the police. Then he ran outside to see if he could help his friend.

Pham blanched at what he saw. The gang had overtaken Hennessee and knocked him to the ground. He lay on the asphalt pavement against the front wheel of a car. Some of the gang members had picked up long, sharp wooden stakes from a flower bed and were hitting Hennessee with them, or jabbing him with the sharp ends. Others were kicking him and beating him with their fists.

Outraged, Pham ran toward the gang. Although he was alone, he decided to try a trick to make the gang think others were with him.

"Come on. This way," he yelled. "Over here. Bob needs our help."

When he was about ten feet away from the gang, he shouted at them to stop.

"Leave him alone. You'd better get out of here, the police are on their way," Pham hollered.

Then a cold shot of fear swept through Pham. The gang turned from Hennessee and started toward him, with the stakes and knives in their hands. One of the gang members swung a stake at Pham's head, but, having studied karate, Pham broke it in half with a chopping blow of his bare hand.

"We're going to get you, wise guy," one of the gang growled. "We're going to skin you alive and then kill you."

Pham carefully threaded his way between cars in the

parking lot, making sure the gang stayed close enough to him so they wouldn't return to continue attacking Hennessee, who had staggered to his feet.

"Help!" Pham yelled. But there was no one to help.

Fearing for his life if the gang caught him, Pham ran 150 feet back into the building, and the gang, afraid of being recognized or being caught, dispersed.

Hennessee, meanwhile, limped to his car and drove to a nearby gas station. An ambulance was called and he was taken to the hospital. His nose had been broken and some of his ribs were cracked, and he had a deep head gash. He had been stabbed four times in the back and once in the leg, both by knives and by the sharpened stakes.

But after five days in the hospital and three weeks at home, he recovered fully. Pham Dang Duoc suffered bruises on his right hand and arm where he had warded off the stake.

Although he was only five feet four inches tall and weighed just 140 pounds, Pham had exhibited a very special kind of courage in facing up to a large gang of armed assailants with no other help and no weapon of his own. His fearless action probably saved Robert Hennessee's life.

☐ Young heroes and heroines are made up of all types of personalities. Many have been class leaders or star athletes. Some are always among the first to take positive action during a situation. But others who may be at the bottom of their classes, or shy and introverted, or even in trouble with the law, have also risen to the occasion when someone's life was in danger.

Such was the case of Hank Rutherford, an eighteen-year-old high school dropout who had been arrested and was being transported in the back seat of a patrol car with another prisoner. In the front seat was deputy sheriff Harold Ewald and another deputy. Both Rutherford and the other prisoner were shackled. But somehow the other man freed his hands, pulled out a knife, and threatened to kill the deputy if Ewald did not stop the car.

As Ewald pulled over to the side of the road, a scuffle began, and the prisoner stabbed the deputy and grabbed his revolver. He then stabbed Ewald, and Ewald turned and shot and wounded the man.

The prisoner then shot Ewald, injuring him. After firing his gun again, Ewald started backing his way out of the car. The prisoner then pointed his revolver directly at Ewald's head.

Fearing that the deputy sheriff would be killed, Hank, still shackled and totally defenseless, lunged against the prisoner and pushed him away from Ewald. Hank then tried to escape out one of the rear doors, but the other prisoner shot him. Then the prisoner flagged down a truck and forced the person inside to drive him away.

The deputy who had been stabbed died from his wounds, but, thanks to Hank Rutherford's alertness and courage, Harold Ewald recovered from his wounds, as did Hank. The prisoner escaped.

12.

Sharks and Grizzly Bears

☐ Almost everyone has a natural fear of certain animals, reptiles, and creatures of the sea. Snakes, for example, send chills of fear up and down the spines of most people. For skin and scuba divers, barracuda and needle-toothed moray eels can make their hair stand on end.

Hunters and trappers will tell you there is nothing more dangerous in the wild than a mad grizzly bear. And divers and swimmers say they fear nothing more than a man-eating shark. Even so, among the Carnegie commission files are cases where teen-agers have challenged the fiercest of wild beasts and the most terrifying of undersea denizens in heroic attempts to save people in trouble.

One of the most dramatic examples occurred in Glacier National Park in eastern British Columbia, Canada. Eighteen-year-old Malcolm Aspeslet and his girl friend, Barbara Beck, were hiking along Balu Pass Trail, enjoying the crisp, clean air on a beautiful fall morning.

Malcolm saw something moving in the brush up ahead and he walked toward it. He smiled. It was a couple of young bear cubs, playfully cuffing each other as they rolled around on the ground.

He was about to call Barbara up to see the cubs, when

she screamed loudly, scaring them off. Malcolm turned around and froze in his tracks. A huge, 800-pound grizzly bear, obviously the mother of the cubs, had rumbled out of the scrubs and was chasing Barbara.

The beast rose up on its hind legs and lashed at her, knocking her hard to the ground. Blood ran down Barbara's forehead and she screamed hysterically.

Momentarily stunned, Malcolm pulled the small hunting knife he carried out of its sheath and ran to help his girl friend. Without thinking of his own safety, he leaped on the great bear's back and began stabbing it in the neck with his knife.

Angered, the bear rose up again and, with a single, sweeping motion of its giant paw, smacked Malcolm off its back, pounding him to the ground and sending the knife sailing off into the bush. The bear turned from Barbara and began attacking Malcolm.

It clawed one side of his face, and its steel jaws clamped down on the top of Malcolm's head. He shrieked in pain. Malcolm tried to wriggle free, but the beast's forepaw slammed down hard on his right arm, breaking it in two places as easily as if it were some brittle twig.

Biting, tearing, white-hot pain seared through Malcolm's body as the grizzly continued its maddened attack, biting into his shoulder and shaking him back and forth as if he were a rag doll. Nearly unconscious, Malcolm stopped trying to escape and lay motionless.

Then, mysteriously, the bear stepped over his inert form and ambled off into the brush. For a moment or two there was a haunting silence. Then Barbara heard Malcolm. She could hardly look at him. He had been badly mauled and was bleeding from a dozen wounds. She knew she had to find the strength somehow to get up and reach help, or he would die.

Painfully, she staggered to her feet. "I'm going for help," she told Malcolm. Numbed by shock, it took her over an hour to reach a ranger station, and, sobbing uncontrollably, she told ranger E. W. Clough her nightmarish story. Clough wasted no time. He ran all the way back to Malcolm. At first he thought he was dead, but he could feel a slight pulse. He applied first aid, and a helicopter was flown in and airlifted Malcolm to a nearby hospital in Revelstoke.

Amazingly, Malcolm recovered. He lost an eye and he underwent skin grafts for plastic surgery for almost two years. It took several operations to repair the damage, but he pulled through and, when last heard from, was planning to marry Barbara, the girl friend whose life he saved by nearly giving up his own.

☐ It was some years before the movie *Jaws* came out that Shirley O'Neill and Albert Kogler, both teen-age students, went swimming in the waters of the Golden Gate in San Francisco, California. They were 150 feet from shore in waters 27 feet deep. No one else was around.

Suddenly Shirley heard Albert scream and she looked over to see a roiling turbulence in the water. He was slashing about madly as he cried for help. Then she realized what was happening. Shark! A large dark-gray shark was attacking Albert. With its massive jaws, it tore out parts of his arm, shoulder, and back, turning the water a dark crimson.

Terrified, Shirley started swimming toward shore. But when she heard Albert crying for help, she turned back. She was terribly afraid, because the water around him was still churning furiously, so she knew the shark was still there. She also feared the blood might attract other sharks.

Nevertheless, finding courage she never knew she

had, Shirley swam directly toward the disturbance in the water. She reached Albert, but couldn't grab hold of his arm or shoulder because they were too badly torn.

"Float on your back if you can," she told him. And he did. She then put her arm across his chest and began swimming with him back toward the beach. It was tough going through swells two feet high, but the current was with them. When they got within sixty feet of the shore, Shirley was nearly exhausted. But then a man on shore cast out a heavy fishing line to her, and she tied it around Albert's good arm and around her own waist. The man then pulled them in, drawing them within twenty-five feet of the shore, where two men waded out and carried Albert in. Shirley stumbled in after them, physically drained.

Albert was rushed to a hospital, but died two hours later.

Because she was fully aware of the great danger involved, yet swam to help her friend even while the shark was still in the water attacking him, Shirley O'Neill was awarded a rare silver medal by the Carnegie Hero Fund Commission.

13.

A Special Kind of "Cool"

☐ Most of the life-saving rescues involving young people are spur-of-the-moment cases. The response is instantaneous. Someone is in trouble. They may be seriously hurt or may die if they are not helped immediately, so action is taken. Most often it happens in seconds, or minutes. A cry from someone flailing about in deep water, or a scream from a person trapped in a burning car . . . this may be all the rescuer sees or hears.

But occasionally a situation comes up where not only must quick action be taken, but also the rescuer or rescuers must do some inventive thinking to save a life or lives. The rescuer must demonstrate extreme coolness in the face of danger and exhibit, at times, a special kind of ingenuity: the rare ability to think imaginatively and resourcefully under a great amount of pressure.

Jared Betts, a sixty-three-year-old clergyman, was fishing one May day in a stream near its junction with Cousins Inlet not far from Ocean Falls, British Columbia. He slipped and fell into the chilled waters and was swept into the inlet. With his clothes soaked and his boots filled with water, Betts was barely able to stay afloat.

"Help!" he called again and again.

Hearing Betts, eleven-year-old Charles Duncan and

his younger brother, Keith, ran to the top of a vertical rock bank rising four feet above the water. Just as they got there, where they had a good view of the inlet, they saw Betts sink beneath the surface.

"We've got to help him," Charles said. "There's no one else around." Swiftly, Charles jumped into the inlet and swam about thirty feet to the point where he had last seen the man. He dived down and brought Betts, who greatly outweighed him, to the surface.

He tried to tow Betts to shore but couldn't make any headway. Keith then dived into the water without even taking off his boots. Together, the two brothers towed Betts thirty feet back to the rock bank. By the time they reached it they were all thoroughly chilled and near exhaustion.

Charles, holding on to Betts, tried to boost Keith up the steep bank, but Keith couldn't quite reach the top.

"What . . . are we going . . . to do?" Keith asked, between deep gasps for breath.

Charles thought for a moment, then said, "I know, Keith. Do you still have your hunting knife with you?" His brother nodded. "Well, see if you can jam it into the bank so we can get a good hold."

Keith took out his knife and wedged it tightly into a small fissure in the rock about two feet above the water. Then he held on to the knife handle with both hands. Betts held on to Keith, and Charles, by holding on to Keith's hands, managed to climb up the bank and out of the water.

Betts then reached up and got hold of Keith's hands, still tightly gripped around the knife, and raised himself enough to place one knee on a narrow ledge. Charles was then able to grab Betts and help him climb out of the water. They both reached down and pulled Keith out.

Charles's quick thinking had saved one and possibly three lives.

☐ When a light plane crashed on a mountain ledge in Alaskan bush country, it overturned and burst into flames. Inside, the pilot was killed. Eighteen-year-old Stephen Herbert had a deep cut across his nose and a wrenched back, but otherwise he seemed okay—no broken bones that he knew of. His father, however, and an Eskimo named Thomas Douglas were seriously injured and could not move.

Recovering quickly from the shock of the crash, Stephen climbed out of his seat and began looking for a fire extinguisher. He couldn't locate one, so he grabbed his father and carried him out of the plane as the flames spread from the engine to the fuselage.

Outside, he heard Douglas calling for help, and he went back in, despite the intense heat and fire. Douglas was suspended head downward with his feet pinned by the instrument panel. Flames were burning around his feet.

Reaching into the cabin, Stephen pulled downward on Douglas's legs and freed one foot, but neither he nor Douglas could move the other one, where the fire had now burned up to his knee. Stephen thought he might have to amputate Douglas's leg if he was to get him out of the plane before he was burned alive, so he got a knife from his father.

Again he entered the white-hot cabin, which was now almost totally enveloped in flames. He dropped down to his knees behind Douglas and pulled as hard as he could on the man's thighs. At last the other leg swung free, although his boot and some flesh had been burned away.

Tired and weak from his effort, Stephen, with great

difficulty, dragged Douglas out of the plane. As they reached the tip of a wing, twenty feet from the cabin, a sudden burst of flames erupted in the fuselage and lashed outward on the wing to within five feet of them.

Within ten minutes, the entire plane had been destroyed, cremating the pilot's body and burning everything inside except a metal survival kit.

Only now did Stephen have time to assess the still-dangerous predicament they were in. His father and Douglas were badly injured and needed immediate medical help. Yet they were isolated on a narrow mountain ledge 3,300 feet above the surrounding ground and forty miles from the nearest settlement.

First Stephen covered Douglas and his father; then he erected a windbreak to ward off the chill mountain winds. As the temperature dropped near freezing, he built a fire to heat stones to warm the two injured men. Next he set his father's broken arm and treated both men with first-aid supplies from the survival kit.

A light snow began to fall as darkness approached, and Stephen sat down, exhausted. Surely, he thought, rescue parties will be sent out in the morning. What can I do to make sure they see us?

When the storm passed, Stephen tramped the word HELP in large letters in the fresh snow. Then, as daylight came, he built a smudge fire, which sent up billows of curling black smoke. And he continued to console and try to help Douglas and his father. There was little more he could do now but wait, and hope.

A short time later, twelve hours after the crash, Stephen heard a welcome sound. At first it was faint and far off, but as it grew stronger he jumped up and began waving his arms frantically. It was a search plane. The pilot had seen the smoke from the smudge fire.

Soon a rescue helicopter arrived and airlifted Stephen, his father, and Douglas to safety. There was hardly a minute to spare, because shortly afterward a heavy blizzard set in, lacing the mountain with high winds and deep snow.

Douglas was hospitalized for five months because of his bad burns, and one leg had to be amputated. Stephen's father was in the hospital for two months. But both recovered thanks to the uncommon resourcefulness and determination of Stephen Herbert.

For his courage, the Carnegie Hero Fund Commission awarded him a silver medal.

14.

Medal Winners Look Back

☐ The act of saving someone's life and the recognition that comes with such an act, through local, regional, and sometimes national publicity, has meant different things to young heroes and heroines.

Most of them, as well as their families and friends, are proud. They are proud of their life-saving rescues and of the recognition and the awarding of the medal. This is especially true with the parents of teen-agers who died in attempts to save others.

Some of the medal recipients are bewildered. They were not fully aware of what they did—dash into a flaming house, or dive into frigid or churning waters—until some time after the rescue had been made. "I can't believe I really did that," some boys and girls have said afterward, as if they had experienced a momentary loss of memory.

A few have expressed embarrassment about the attention given their act. None of the young heroes and heroines even thought about publicity or awards when they risked their lives to save others. And for a few, the handling of such adoration and attention has been difficult.

Most young Carnegie medal winners just feel that what they did was something that had to be done. A person was in trouble and needed help and they helped. They view it as simply as that.

Conversation and correspondence with a number of heroes and heroines, many of them represented in this book, plus some others, reveals a diversity of thoughts regarding the various aspects of their individual rescues.

"A lot of things were going through my head," recalls Bill Welch, Jr., who saved sixty-year-old Phil Williamson from his flaming ice cream truck after it had been demolished by a freight train.

"I just couldn't stand the thought of a man burning up. No one else was doing anything, so I felt I had to. I asked the Lord to help me.

"The medal award meant a lot to me," Bill says. "It's hard to express it in words, but it was a tremendous aid to me. The act gave me a great deal of confidence in myself to know I could react this way."

"The award itself has meant many different things to me; primarily it has given me a new picture of myself," says Arthur Yost III of Gloversville, New York. When eighty-one-year-old Mrs. Agnes Krause lost control of her car, and it plunged into a millpond and began to sink at the front end in deep water forty feet from the bank, Arthur swam to the car, pulled Mrs. Krause from it, and towed her to the bank.

"The act of saving a person's life in time was something I didn't know that I could do until I did it. Mostly, I want to thank my parents for teaching me the values of being unselfish, respecting other people, and helping them in their time of need even if I sacrifice something of my own," Arthur says.

Karen Edwards, the thirteen-year-old schoolgirl who saved Eugene Taylor and his son from drowning in a motel swimming pool, says, "Rescuing somebody is the hardest thing to do. You have a tendency to panic. And knowing that your life may be taken makes it even harder. You must try not to panic and have confidence in yourself. The Carnegie Hero award is something I will always remember and be thankful for."

Brent Gough, who rescued a man in Maui, Hawaii, from drowning in rough surf, remembers, "When I heard him call for help, I just dove in and swam as fast as I could. During the rescue, the man panicked, making it difficult to help him. At first I felt confident that I could get him to safety, but soon found myself exhausted and in trouble too. I think I was more scared than he was. My calls for help were muffled by the crash of the surf. I guess it was the worst experience of my life.

"I had not really thought about my personal feelings toward the award," Brent says. "It is very difficult to answer. The award has meant a great deal to me and I appreciated it very much. While going to school the students and the teachers had a whole new outlook toward me, which has helped a great deal to get ahead in life."

Ric Courson, who helped save several children from drowning when a bridge collapsed, hurling them into churning flood waters in Ohio, says, "I feel good about what I did. I'm proud of the medal, but to me it's like a soldier coming back from the war with a purple heart. He doesn't wear it. He puts it in a box and puts it away. And it's his memory. I don't talk about it today, but the experience is something that will stay with me for the rest of my life."

Adds Ronald Barreras, the teen-ager who lost a leg saving a girl on horseback from being struck by a train, "It [the rescue] gave me a feeling of satisfaction, and what better feeling could you have? I don't know if there are

"Greater love hath no man than this: that a man lay down his life for his friends—"
John, 15:13

any people who feel sorry for themselves because of permanent damage to their body. But that's one feeling I don't have. And I don't like anyone feeling sorry for me, because I would never be able to enjoy life like I normally would if they did.

"The only advice I have for others is to stay calm and don't panic. Panic is the main cause of deaths in this kind of situation."

Gene Miller, the student who chased across a busy highway and ran down a runaway car with a child inside, recalls, "Everything happened so fast it's hard to remember. I could see the child's head and I thought to myself, 'Oh, my God, it's getting away.' I then started sprinting after it. When the car threw me at the median strip, I got up and said to myself, 'Got to get it.' I then continued running after it. After the car was finally stopped, I got out and exclaimed, 'I don't believe it!'"

Gene feels three things can happen to young people who find themselves in a crisis situation. "One thing you can do is panic," he says. "This makes the situation even harder and it could prove fatal. So the worst thing to do is panic.

"The second thing is the most important thing to remember: think quickly. This makes the situation more orderly and it protects you and others from getting hurt. The third thing that could happen is that you react instinctively. Not everyone can do this. If you do react in this manner, you still must think in order to keep from getting hurt or having anyone else get hurt.

"The main thing to remember," Gene says, "is to give aid to a person who is in need of help, even if you have to get others to help also.

"The Carnegie Hero award has bestowed a great

honor upon me that I will cherish for all of my life. From receiving this award I have learned to help people whenever possible, even if it is just a small little favor. Because there is always a chance that you will need their help one day."

About the Author

☐ L. B. Taylor, Jr. first became interested in the Carnegie Hero Fund Commission when he was asked to write a magazine article. Author of over two hundred articles and six books, Mr. Taylor has been associated with the aerospace and chemical industries.

L. B. Taylor, Jr. is presently Public Relations Director for a large fiber and chemical firm near his home in Williamsburg, Virginia. He is also the author of CHEMISTRY CAREERS (A Career Concise Guide) for Franklin Watts.